Wolf howls at the moon.
His mysterious song soars
Across the night sky.
by J.E. Moore

Wolves Are

Wolves are...
Wild things
Free things
Moving, running, healthy — free.

Wolves are...
Loving things
Family things
Devoted, loyal, loving — warm.

Wolves are...
Lovely things
Stately things
Furry, strong, graceful — beautiful.

Wolves are...
Smart things
Cunning things
Sly, artful, hunters — intelligent.

Wolves are not...
Murdering things
Purposefully mean things,
Ugly, fierce, hateful things — killers.

But

Wolves are...
Hunted things,
Trapped things,
Stalked, snared, captured — killed.

by Leslie Tryon

Wolves

Let's Learn About Wolves

Books About Wolves:

Non-Fiction

Baby Wolf by Beth Spanjian; Longmeadow Press, 1988 (Grade 2)

Small Wolf by Nathaniel Benchley; Harper & Row Junior Books (Grade 2)

Wild Dog (a Zoobook) by Timothy Levi Biel; Wildlife Education, Ltd., 1986 (Grades 2-4)

National Geographic Book of Mammals, Volume 2; National Geographic Society, 1981 (Wolves can be found on pages 583 to 588) (Grades 2-4)

Wolf Pack, Tracking Wolves in the Wild by Sylvia A. Johnson and Alice Aamodt; Lerner Publications Company, 1985 (Grade 4 — This book has excellent material that can be shared with grades 2 and 3, but will need paraphrasing by the teacher.)

Wolves (a Zoobook) by Timothy Levi Biel; Wildlife Education, Ltd., 1986 (Grades 2-4)

Wolves by Betty Polisar Reigot; Scholastic Book Services, 1980 (Grades 2-4)

Fiction

Great Wolf and the Good Woodsman by Helen Hoover; Parents' Magazine Press, 1967 (Grades 2-4)

Little Red Riding Hood by Trina Schart Hyman; Holiday House, 1983 (Grades 2-4)

The Three Little Pigs by Joseph Jacobs; G.P. Putnam's Sons, 1980 (Grades 2-4)

The Wolf's Chicken Stew by Keika Kasza; Putnam, 1987 (Grade 2)

The Wounded Wolf by Jean Craighead George; Harper and Row, 1978 (Grades 3-4)

Before We Begin

What we know about wolves.	What we want to learn about wolves.

Wolves

What is a wolf? Well, a wolf is a wild dog. A dog very much like the pet dogs we have at home. Wolves are smart. They are friendly and playful — with other wolves of course! They are loyal to the members of their pack, just as your pet dog is loyal to you and your family.

Wolves can be found in North America, Europe, and Asia. There are not as many wolves around as there once were. Many have been killed by hunters and in many areas their habitats have been taken over by farming and the development of cities. Look at the map on the next page. At one time gray wolves could be found almost all over North America. Now they can be found only in the areas shown on the map.

Look carefully at the map. Which state in the U.S.A. has the largest area where wolves can be found? Color that state red.

Why do you think there are more wolves in this state than in the rest of the United States?

The range of the gray wolf, canis lupis, in North America.

What Does a Wolf Look Like?

Wolves come in many different colors and sizes.

The fur on an animal such as a wolf is called its pelage. A wolf may have hairs of several different colors on its body. In fact, not all gray wolves are colored gray. The markings can be different also. The colors and markings can help the wolf seem to blend in with the background. This makes it difficult for an enemy to see the wolf. Pups born in the same litter may have different colored fur.

A male wolf can weigh from 70 pounds (32 kilograms) to as much as 100 pounds (45 kilograms). He can measure from 5 feet (1.5 meters) to 6½ feet (1.9 meters). Females are smaller than the males. A female may weigh between 55 pounds (24 kilograms) and 90 pounds (41 kilograms). She may reach a length of 4½ feet (1.3 meters) to 6 feet (1.8) meters.

Color the wolves on this page.

A Wolf's Body

A wolf's eyesight is not as good as its other senses. A wolf will often smell something long before he sees it. A wolf has such a good sense of smell, he can smell prey more than a mile (1.6 km) away.

A wolf's sense of hearing is so good, he can hear other wolves howling several miles away. A wolf's ears turn from side to side so he can tell the direction a sound is coming from without having to turn his head.

Wolves have strong muscles and long legs for running. They run on their toes. This makes them run even faster.

Wolves have strong jaws and sharp teeth to help them hold and tear their prey. The long, pointed teeth (canines) in front are for grabbing and holding. The teeth in the wolf's jaw (carnassial) slice food into small pieces so the wolf can swallow it. The small teeth in front (incisors) pick meat off of the bones.

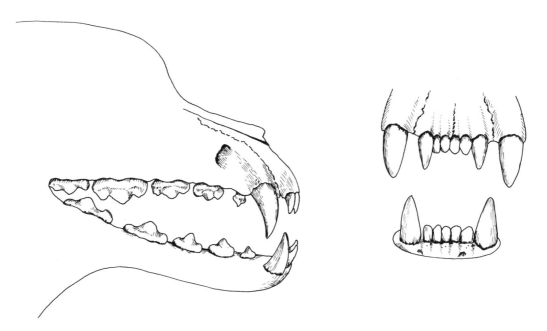

Think about how you use your teeth to eat.

● Which teeth do you use to tear meat off of a chicken bone?

● Which teeth do you use to grind up the vegetables you eat?

● Do you have any sharp pointed teeth?

Try running on your toes. Does it make you faster or slower?

How Do Wolves Talk to Each Other?

Wolves have two ways to "talk" to each other.

Wolves use sounds. They howl, whimper, whine, growl, and bark. This lets the members of the pack know how they feel and what they want. These sounds also help warn enemies to stay away.

Wolves use "body language" to show how they feel. The way the wolf holds its ears, hair, tail, and teeth carry messages to other wolves.

What do you think these wolves are saying?

Think About It:

How does your pet use sounds and its body to tell you what it wants?

How do you use "body language" to show how you feel?

Dinner Time

Wolves are carnivores. This means they are meat eaters. They are also called predators. This means they hunt and kill their food. Wolves hunt in a pack. When a wolf has to hunt alone, it captures smaller prey such as mice and rabbits. But to feed the whole pack, wolves need to catch large prey. By working together and using their brains, good hearing and sense of smell, speed, and strength, they can kill prey as large as a moose. All of the animals in the pack share this food.

Circle the pictures of food a wolf would eat.

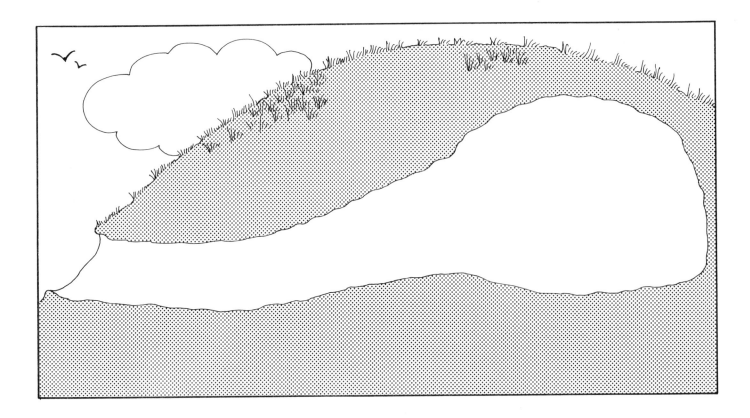

A Litter of Pups

Wolves are very good parents. They feed and protect their babies until they are grown. Wolf pups are born in the spring. The litter of pups are born underground in a den. The pups are tiny and helpless when they are born. Their eyes are closed and they cannot walk. Mother wolf nurses them. This means she feeds them milk from her own body.

The pups grow very fast. By two weeks their eyes are open and they can walk around. After three weeks they begin to come out of the den to play, but they stay close to the opening. At about ten weeks they leave the den and live with the rest of the pack.

After a few weeks of only milk, the pups begin to be fed meat. The adults carry meat back from the hunt in their stomachs. The pups lick the jaws of an adult. This causes the adult to bring the food back up into its mouth so it can be fed to the pups.

By three months old the pups look like adults, but they don't begin to hunt until they are about six months old.

Draw wolf pups in the den at the top of this page.

Note: Each child will need a sheet of paper and a copy of this page. The pictures may be pasted in the correct order on unlined paper or they may be pasted down the side of a sheet of writing paper and used for sentence or paragraph writing.

Wolf Life Cycle

Color   Cut apart   Paste in the correct order.

Note: This is another way to practice sequencing events. Have the children number the sentences in the correct order. It is easier for some children to cut the sentences apart and paste them in the correct order on a second sheet of paper.

The Life Cycle of the Gray Wolf

_____ Wolf pups are small and helpless when they are born.

_____ Pups can now play around the opening to their den.

_____ After a few months, the pups leave the den and stay at resting sites with a "pup-sitter" while the rest of the pack is hunting.

_____ Some of the grown wolves will stay with the pack; others will go off to form new packs and have pups of their own.

_____ Pups drink their mother's milk soon after they are born.

_____ The pups begin to eat meat regurgitated by the other wolves.

_____ At six months the young wolves begin to learn how to hunt.

_____ After a few weeks, the pups open their eyes and begin to walk around.

A Pack of Wolves

Wolves like to live in a group. This group is called a pack. A pack is made up of a father and mother wolf, their pups, and some other relatives. The wolves in a pack are loyal to each other. They live, hunt, and play together.

There is a special way wolves are grouped that helps keep pack members from fighting with each other. This is important since wolves are so strong they could hurt each other. Each wolf has a special rank in the group. The leader is usually the largest, strongest wolf. Other wolves are lower in rank. The way a wolf holds its ears and tail show its rank in the group. The lower ranking wolves treat those above them with respect. When two wolves do disagree, they bare their teeth and snarl at each other trying to look fierce. Usually the one with lower rank will roll over on its back to show that it gives up.

Think About It:

How is a class of students similar to a "pack"?

13

Wolf to Pet

How did the wild wolf become the lovable pet dog we know today?
No one knows for sure, but it may have happened this way...

Long, long ago wolves sometimes followed hunters at a safe distance.
When the hunters left, the wolves would eat the scraps of meat left
behind. These early men noticed how brave and intelligent the wolves
were. Some humans began to take wolf pups and raise them to be
watch dogs and to help hunt. Wolves like to live and work in groups.
They looked at the humans that raised them as their pack leader.

Over thousands of years, these early "pets" have become the dogs
that are our pets today.

Choose a partner. Pretend you were that early hunter. What would
you do to turn the wild wolf pup into a pet? (You may want to write
your plan on the form on the next page.)

 Wolves

The First Pet Dog

Wolves

Cave Pet
A Skit

The little cave child inside the cave and the wolf pup outside the cave in the cold and the wind, study each other and wonder what it would be like to know one another. Since no child can resist a puppy and no puppy can resist a child, they decide to be pals. The child speaks first and then the wolf. The speaking parts go back and forth between the two characters.

BOY OR GIRL   **WOLF**

BOY OR GIRL	WOLF
I'm lonely. I guess I'll just sit by the fire.	I think it must be dangerous in there; I see a fire.
Besides, it's really cold outside.	It looks nice and warm in that cave and it's cold out here.
(Finishing up a piece of meat, he tosses the bone aside.) I'm full.	I'm hungry. I wonder if he would share that bone with me?
I wish I could clean this grease off my hands.	I could show him how to lick his hands clean.
(Yawning) I'm sleepy. Mom and Dad are off on a hunt and I have to sleep all alone.	My pack has all gone off on a hunt. I don't have anyone to sleep with. I'm cold.
(Looking at the wolf pup and thinking out loud) I wonder if he's lonely too.	(Looking back at the boy) I think he must be lonely too. He doesn't have anyone around.

Boy or Girl

Maybe he would come in here if I offered him this bone.

(Cave child offers the bone.)
Come on boy, you don't have to be afraid. We can keep each other company.

(The cave boy carefully strokes the wolf pup.) This is nice. I've never been this close to an animal before.

In the morning we could go out and play. I could show him how to fetch.

I trust you. I'm going to go to sleep now.

Wolf

He looks young like me. I don't think I'm afraid of him.

(The wolf pup enters the cave very carefully, looking side to side, and behind himself. He keeps an eye on the fire.)
He's offering me that bone. It's warm in here — how nice.

This is nice. I've never been this close to a human before. I've never let one touch me.

We could go out and play in the morning. I could show him how I can catch.

I think I trust you. I'll just curl up next to you and we'll both stay warm.

This play is a good lead-in to discussions on several levels. You may want to take time to guide your students to reaching these understandings:

1. The two learned a great deal about each other just by observing. They communicated without spoken language.
2. They were each very careful not to frighten each other. They decided to trust each other once their fear was gone.
3. Having a pet, just like having a friend, is about responsibility and trust.

Wolf Stick Puppet

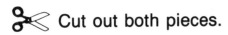 Cut out both pieces.

Color with crayons or marking pens.

Tape or paste the
snout to the face.

Attach a tongue depressor
to the back.

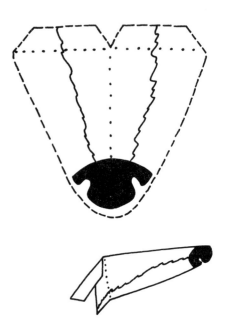

Wolf Mask

Materials:

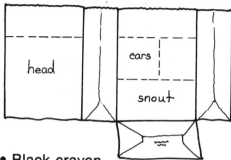

- Large brown paper bag

- Black crayon
- Yarn or string

Steps to follow:

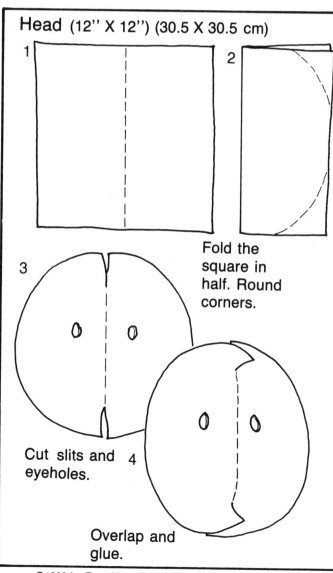

Head (12'' X 12'') (30.5 X 30.5 cm)

1

2

Fold the square in half. Round corners.

3

Cut slits and eyeholes.

4

Overlap and glue.

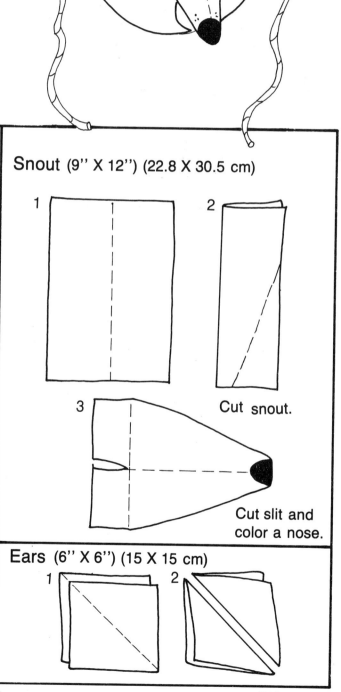

Snout (9'' X 12'') (22.8 X 30.5 cm)

1

2

Cut snout.

3

Cut slit and color a nose.

Ears (6'' X 6'') (15 X 15 cm)

1

2

Wolves

Wolf or Dog?

If it is true about wolves, write wolf on the line.

If it is true about dogs, write dog on the line.

If it's true about dogs and wolves then write both.

1. a wild animal

2. a domestic animal

3. a carnivore

4. helpless at birth

5. a very smart animal

6. born in a den underground

7. guards its owner's home

8. hunts in a pack

9. has sharp teeth for tearing meat

10. marks its territory

Compare and Contrast
A Wolf and a Person

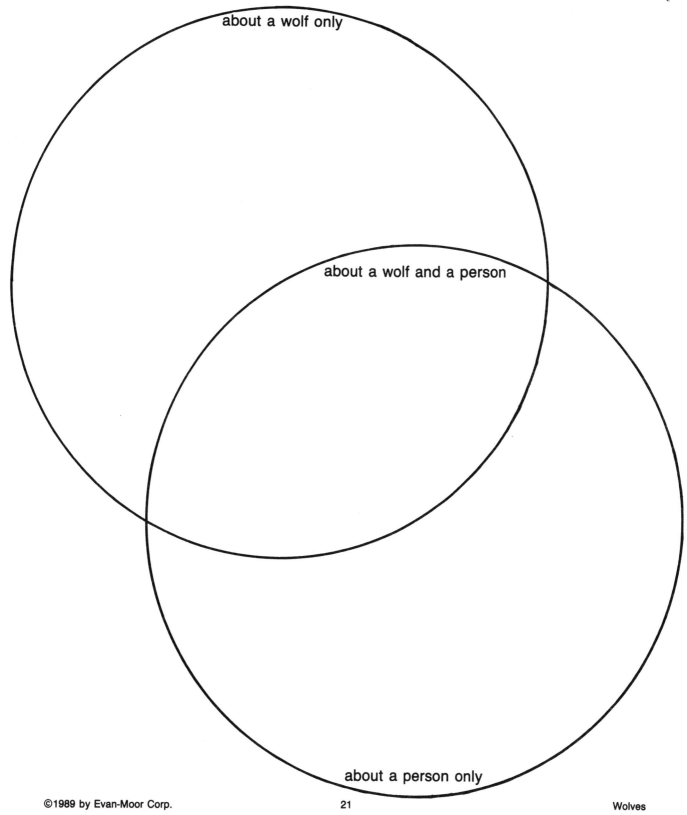

about a wolf only

about a wolf and a person

about a person only

Wolves

Wild Dogs Around the World

Wolves are wild dogs. There are other wild dogs around the world. Where do these wild dogs live?

dingo -

fennec -

bush dog -

coyote -

raccoon dog -

dhole -

maned wolf -

jackal -

Dogs — Wild and Pet

A wolf is a wild dog.
List other wild dogs.

A poodle is a pet dog.
List other pet dogs.

1. _____

2. _____

3. _____

4. _____

5. _____

6. _____

7. _____

8. _____

9. _____

10. _____

1. _____

2. _____

3. _____

4. _____

5. _____

6. _____

7. _____

8. _____

9. _____

10. _____

     Wolves

Fact or Opinion?

fact	opinion	
☐	☐	Wolves are bad because they kill other animals.
☐	☐	Wolves sometimes kill cattle.
☐	☐	Wolves should never be killed by hunters.
☐	☐	Wolves are beautiful.
☐	☐	Wolves live in packs.
☐	☐	Wolves take good care of their pups.
☐	☐	Wolves are really harmful to cattle and sheep.
☐	☐	All wolves are good hunters.
☐	☐	Wolves can live in many different habitats.
☐	☐	Wolves are the smartest of the wild animals.
☐	☐	All pet dogs are descended from wolves.
☐	☐	Wolves are better hunters than lions.

Think of an opinion about wolves.

_____

_____

_____

Think of a fact about wolves.

_____

_____

_____

Words About Wolves

Write the correct word on each wolf's tail.
Use these words to help you find the answers.

den	pup	wolf
litter	teeth	fur
pack	wild	mammal

a group of wolves

pups born at the same time

the hair on a wolf

baby wolves are born in a _____

wolves have sharp _____

a baby wolf

Note: Have students look up the meaning of any word they do not know before working the crossword. You will need to help younger and less able students with some of the vocabulary.

What Does It Mean?

cache
canidae
carnivores
den
digitigrade
fur
litter
mammals
nurse
pack
pelage
predator
pup
territory
werewolf
wild

Across

2. a spot where meat is buried near the den
7. another name for animal hair
9. meat-eaters
11. hairy covering for a wolf's body
12. puppies born at the same time to the same mother
13. area where a pack of wolves hunts and lives
14. opposite of tame
15. furry animals whose babies are born live

Down

1. baby wolves are born in a _____
3. scientific name for wolves
4. when a mother feeds milk to her baby
5. the word for how a wolf runs on its toes
6. a group of wolves that live together
8. an animal that hunts and kills for food
10. a fictional human that turns into a wolf
11. a baby wolf

Wolves

Wild Dog Word Search

```
A R C T I C F O X W O L F D
R F Z W O L F D J P U P W I
A G R A Y F O X O A X U O N
C P E I N G P Z W G C P L G
C U D W C X R U D O P K F O
O P F O O A Q A P O L U A X
O R O L Y P N V Y R G F P L
N E X F O U Z W U W T Z W B
D D W G T P J K I D O G O U
O W O F E N N E C L Z L L S
G O L P U P W O L F D R F H
R L F A D H O L E B V D X D
Z F X M A N E D W O L F O O
B A T E A R E D F O X W Z G
```

AFRICAN WILD DOG
ARCTIC FOX
BAT-EARED FOX
BUSH DOG
COYOTE
DHOLE
DINGO
FENNEC
GRAY FOX
GRAY WOLF
JACKAL
MANED WOLF
RACCOON DOG
RED FOX
RED WOLF

How many times can you find WOLF? _____

Wolves

Dot-to-Dot

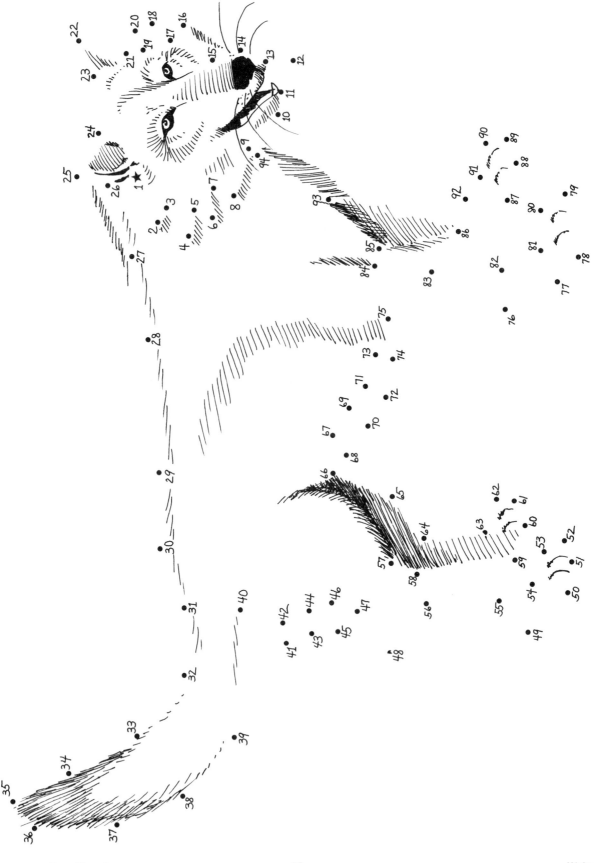

28

Wolves

Note: Practice using an information chart to answer questions. The sizes listed are averages. Be sure that children realize that some measurements are in inches (centimeters) and others are in feet (meters). You may cover up either set of numbers if you feel it is confusing to your students to see both.

Compare the Sizes of Wild Dogs

	Body		Tail	
gray wolf	4'	(1.2 m)	15''	(38 cm)
fennec	15''	(38 cm)	7¾''	(20 cm)
dingo	5'	(1.5 m)	13¾''	(34 cm)
coyote	35½''	(90 cm)	13½''	(34 cm)
red fox	24''	(60 cm)	17''	(42 cm)

1. Which wild dog has the longest tail? _____

2. Which wild dog has the shortest body? _____

3. How many wild dogs are listed on the chart? _____

4. How long is the tail of a coyote? _____

5. How long is the body of a red fox? _____

6. Which wild dog has a body that is four feet (1.2 meters) long?

_____

7. Which wild dog has a tail that is 17'' (42 cm) long? _____

8. How much longer is the body of a dingo than the body of a gray wolf?

_____

9. How much shorter is the tail of a gray wolf than the tail of a red fox?

_____

10. Which has a longer tail, a coyote or a dingo? _____

11. Which has a shorter body, a fennec or a red fox? _____

12. What is the total length of the body and tail of a . . . . ?

gray wolf _____

fennec _____

red fox _____

Note: Reproduce these pictures to use when you need realistic representations of wild dogs.

Wild Dogs

Dhole

Maned Wolf

Raccoon Dog

Coyote

Jackal

Wolves

Dingo

Bush Dog

Fennec Fox

Gray Wolf

Red Fox

Wolf — Wolves

One is a ...   More than one are...

coyote

sheep

fox

mouse

octopus

calf

horse

pony

goose

deer

goat

ox

Wolves

Note: These may be done orally or in written form. They may be done by the whole class, in cooperative learning groups, or put on cards for a free-time activity.

Wondering About Wolves

Think about the question. Try to support your answer with facts.

- -

 Should some areas be kept wild for endangered animals such as wolves? Why or why not? What if the land is needed to grow food or for new homes?

- -

 Is a wolf a good or a bad animal? Can we judge animal behavior by human rules?

- -

 Why are wolves so often villains in stories? (For example – Little Red Riding Hood)

- -

 What does the saying "a wolf in sheep's clothing" mean?

- -

 What would the earth be like if all predators disappeared?

- -

Note: This activity is designed to help children create more interesting sentences. You may want to put the finished sentences in the three-fold book on the following page to produce a class book for everyone to share.

The wolf howled.

Categories — Select three or more categories depending on the level of your students. Always include adjective, noun, and verb.

Brainstorm — Fill in one category at a time beginning with describing words. List the children's suggestions on the chalkboard or on a chart. (Older children may want to use a dictionary at this point to find more challenging words.)

describing words:	did what?:	where?:	when?:
mighty	snarled	along the river bank	long ago
fierce	sniffed the air	deep in the forest	when the deer fell
gray	tracked his prey	in the cozy den	in the spring
old	nuzzled her pups	at the edge of the canyon	every day
courageous	escaped from the trap	under the big rock	at sunset

	describing words		did what?	where?	when?
The	mighty	wolf	sniffed the air	deep in the forest	at sunset

Oral Sentences

Allow time for children to create many oral sentences using the words and phrases on the chalkboard. This modeling is especially important for hesitant writers.

Write

Have the children select one word or phrase from each column to create interesting sentences.

> The watchful wolf howled to warn the pack of danger one dark, lonely night.
> The frisky, little pup stuck his nose out of the den to see what was going on.

Wolves

What is in the Den?
A Three-Fold Book Cover

Materials:

    6" X 18" (15.24 X 45.7 cm)
    brown construction paper
    crayons or marking pens
    scissors

Follow these steps:

    Fold in thirds.

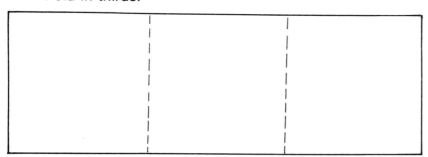 

    Round corners.

 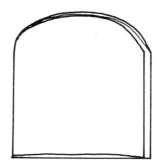

    Draw pictures.

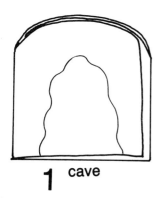

1 cave

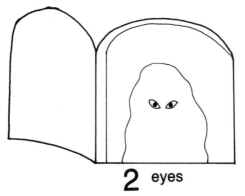

2 eyes

3 Write.
Draw pup.

Use for...
Poems
Descriptive paragraphs
Riddles

     35   Wolves

Once Upon a Time

Write your own story about a wolf adventure.

- Plan your story before you begin to write. Think about...

    1. Your characters
    2. The problem your wolf must solve
    3. The solution (it must make sense!)

- Write your story.

- Proof for mistakes and make a final copy.

- Illustrate the story.

    Sample Story Titles:

    The Lost Wolf Pup
    If I Were A Wolf
    Why Wolves Howl at the Moon
    Escape from the Zoo
    The Wolf Who Could Talk
    My First Hunt
    Who's the Boss?

Draw a Wolf

Standing

Sitting

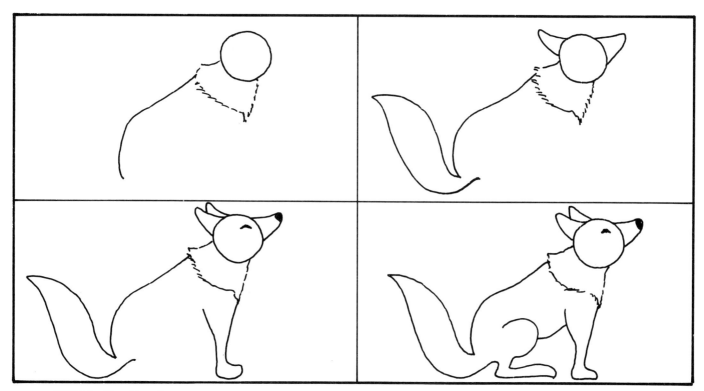

Note: Guide students through the steps for creating any kind of poem until they become comfortable with the form. Then have them write independently.

Wolf Songs

Encourage your students to write poems (rhyming or not) explaining why a wolf might howl at the moon.

Brainstorm to create a list of feelings that might lead a wolf to howl. For example...

happy   angry   curious   fearful   lonely   cautious

Set a pattern to follow in writing the verse. (More experienced ''poets'' may not need this step.) For example:

Why does a wolf howl at the moon?

(stomach full)

_____

(pack safe)

_____

(he sings a contented tune)

_____

That is why a wolf howls at the moon.

Allow time for writing and re-writing.

Display the finished poems for everyone to enjoy.

Note: Use the form on the following page for the basic pop-up form. Select as few or as many topics as are appropriate for your class. You may want to make it a "guided" book with second graders or less able students.

My Wolf Report
A Pop-Up Book

Have your students create their own pop-up books about wolves.

Give them as many pages as they need. Have them write and draw before doing any of the cutting and folding.

Writing— Students write about one topic on each page. Here are two sample formats you might follow:

1. Fill in the blank with a word or phrase.

A wolf is _____.

Wolves hunt for food. They eat _____.

Baby wolves are born alive. They _____.

2. Set a topic. Students write a paragraph on that topic.

Description of a Wolf   Raising a Litter of Pups
Where Wolves Live   Communication
The Wolf Pack   The Future for Wolves
Food for Wolves

Making pop-up pages—

Guide students through the following cuts and folds to create the pop-up tabs on their story pages.

Draw the wolf on the tab. Write the

 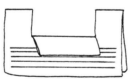 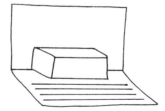 

information on the lines.

Paste the pages together as shown.

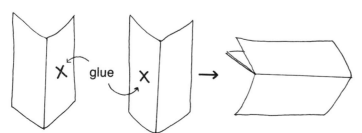

Paste the pages into a cover made from folded construction paper.

Wolves

Note: Follow the directions on the preceding page to create a pop-up page.

Fold

Fold

cut

Draw here.

cut

Fold

Bulletin Boards

A Pack of Good Work

1. Cover the bulletin board area with construction paper.
2. Make wolf masks following the directions on page 19.
3. Pin the wolves to the board. Add children's work.
4. Add a title cut from yellow construction paper.

What do you know about wolves?

1. Cover the bulletin board area with yellow construction paper.
2. Make the wolf pups on page 42.
3. Write a statement about wolves in a speech bubble for each pup.

 Wolves

Pattern for Pup

Reproduce the head on construction paper. Follow the directions below to make the body and tail.

How to cut the body.	How to cut the tail.

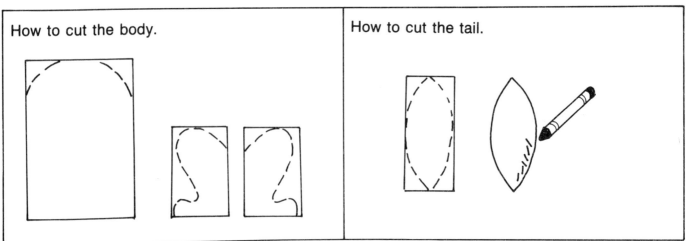

42

Wolves

Note: These activities may be done orally or in written form. They may be done by individual students, in cooperative-learning groups, or as whole-class experiences.

Open-Ended Activities to Use With Books About Wolves

Re-tell the story:

- in outline form
- in the "5 Ws" form (who, did what, where, when, why)
- in paragraph form using your own words
- as a short play, puppet show, radio show, etc.
- in a comic book format
- setting it in a new location or time period

Describe:

- a character from the story
- a setting or location important to the story
- a feeling or mood
- one particular event

Find examples of:

- cause and effect
- fact or fiction
- figures of speech
- descriptive language

Compare and contrast:

- characters within the story
- two books with a similar theme
- two books by the same author or illustrator

Share the book with others:

- give a book talk
- write a book review
- create an advertisement
- make a new book cover

 Wolves

Note: Read one or more versions of this story to your class. (Older students may want to read the story on their own.) The same activities may be used with any of your favorite wolf stories.

Little Red Riding Hood
A Book Project

True or Make-Believe? — Have your students work together to create two lists. Make one list of what could be true in the story and a second list of what could not be true.

Re-write the story — Children may work in a group, in pairs, or as individuals to retell this familiar story. Children ready for a greater challenge might try to ...

        write the story from the wolf's point of view

        write a new version set in a different time period or area

        write part of the story in rhyme

Pop-Up Wolf — Guide students through these steps to make a pop-up wolf. Each child will need a copy of the pattern on the following page.

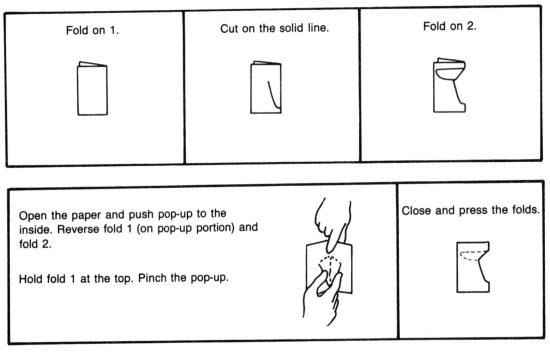

Draw the wolf around the snout on the pop-up form.
Paste the pop-up inside a construction paper folder.

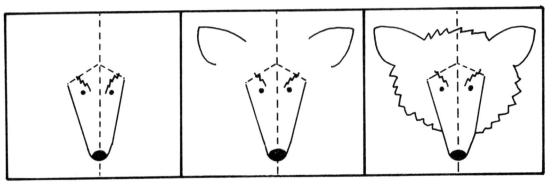

Wolf Pattern

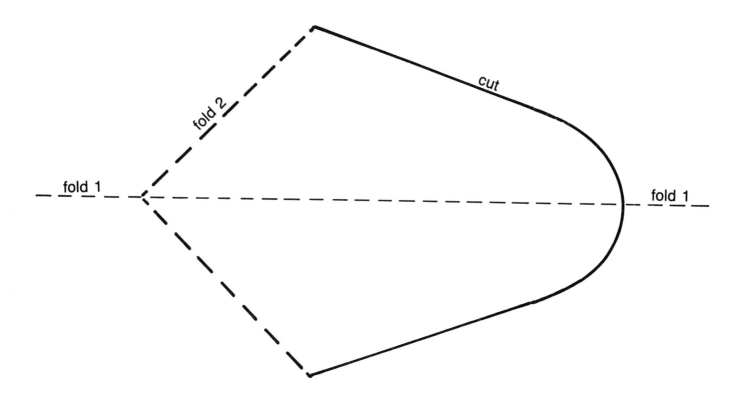

fold 2

cut

fold 1

fold 1

Wolves

Note: The next three pages contain blank wolf forms that can be used in many different ways across the curriculum.

Using Wolf Activity Sheet Patterns

Page 47

- vocabulary lists of wolf words
- spelling words appropriate to the wolf unit
- words for a dictionary search activity
- homework assignments for a week
- language challenges

Page 48

- a math problem in each small wolf
    computation
    counting challenges
    word problems
- riddles
- matching activities
- name tags or labels for folders/reports

Page 49

- write descriptive paragraphs or original poems
- handwriting practice
- cover art for a report or storybook
- list wolf books read during the unit

Wolves

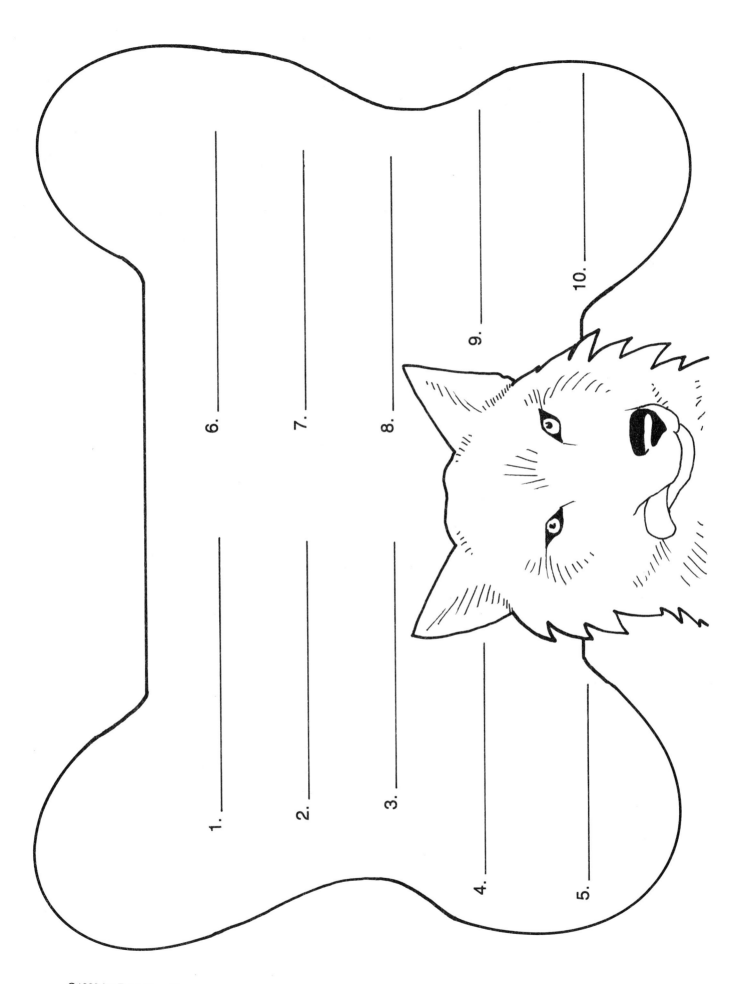

1. _____

2. _____

3. _____

4. _____

5. _____

6. _____

7. _____

8. _____

9. _____

10. _____

Wolves

Wolves